Age Happens

The Best Quotes About Growing Older

Selected by Bruce Lansky

Meadowbrook Press
Distributed by Simon & Schuster
New York, NY

Library of Congress Cataloging-in-Publication Data

Age happens : the best quotes about growing older / selected by Bruce Lansky.
          p.   cm.
      Includes index.
      1. Old age—Quotations, maxims, etc.   2. Aging—Quotations, maxims, etc.
   I. Lansky, Bruce
   PN6084.05A43   1996
   305.26—dc20
                                                    95-44800
                                                    CIP

ISBN: 0-88166-244-5
Simon & Schuster Ordering # 671-56112-X

Editor: Bruce Lansky
Editorial Coordinator: David Tobey
Production Manager: Amy Unger
Desktop Publishing Manager/Text Design: Jay Hanson
Electronic Prepress Manager/Cover Design: Linda Norton

Cartoons: p. xi Drawing by Lorenz, © 1972 *The New Yorker* Magazine, Inc.; p. 7 Drawing by M. Twohy, © 1980 *The New Yorker* Magazine, Inc.; pp. 12, 30, 45, 85, 88 © *The Saturday Evening Post*; p. 17 © 1966 by *Medical Economics*; pp. 22, 40, 65, 100 © 1991 Ed Fischer; p. 27 © Lynn Johnston; p. 34 © 1995 Ed Fischer; p. 48 Drawing by W. Miller, © 1994 *The New Yorker* Magazine, Inc.; p. 55 Crankshaft © Mediagraphics, Inc. Reprinted with permission of Universal Press Syndicate. All rights reserved; p. 60 Drawing by Frascino, © 1980 *The New Yorker* Magazine, Inc.; p. 70 © Steven Carpenter; p. 76 © 1995 by Lawrence W. Harris; p. 81 © Dave Carpenter; p. 95 Drawing by Peter Arno © 1963, 1991 *The New Yorker* Magazine, Inc.

Poems: p. 10 poem by Ogden Nash reprinted with permission of Curtis Brown Ltd. Copyright © 1955 by Ogden Nash, renewed; p. 79 © 1996 by Bruce Lansky. Used with permission of the author; p. 83 copyright © 1992 by William R. Evans III and Andrew Frothingham; p. 98 poem "Thought For a Sunshiny Morning" by Dorothy Parker, from *The Portable Dorothy Parker,* Introduction by Brendan Gill. Copyright 1928, renewed © 1956 by Dorothy Parker. Used with permission of Viking Penguin, a division of Penguin Books USA Inc.

Epigrams: pp. 28, 31 © Ashleigh Brilliant, Santa Barbara, CA. Used with permission of the author.

Published by Meadowbrook Press, 5451 Smetana Drive, Minnetonka, MN 55343

BOOK TRADE DISTRIBUTION by Simon & Schuster, a division of Simon and Schuster, Inc., 1230 Avenue of the Americas, New York, NY 10020

03 02   15 14 13

Printed in the United States of America.

CONTENTS

ACKNOWLEDGMENTS

We would like to thank the individuals who served on a reading panel for this project:

Susan D. Anderson, Shirley Bingham, Betsy Franco, Charles Ghigna, Babs Bell Hajdusiewicz, Dick Hayman, Bobbi Katz, Jo S. Kittinger, Sydnie Meltzer Kleinhenz, Kim Koehler, Helen Ksypka, Charlene Meltzer, Rolaine Merchant, Lois Muehl, Lorraine Bates-Noyes, Claire Puneky, Mickey Schantz, Robert Scotellaro, Sherri Shunfenthal, Nancy Sweetland, Denise Tiffany, Esther Towns, and Penny Warner.

INTRODUCTION

At most birthday parties I've attended for adults over the age of twenty-nine, after "Happy Birthday to You" and "How Old Are You?" have been sung ad nauseum, an awkward moment comes when someone really should say something clever before all the old fogies in attendance fall asleep for lack of aural stimulation.

This is the book for that moment. In it, you will find words of wit and wisdom about:

- why youth is wasted on the young
- the value of experience
- the meaning of life
- why death is really not all that bad (considering the grief your loved ones subject you to)

You can use the quotes, jokes, and rhymes in these pages to dress up an otherwise dull speech. Or, simply pass the book around to anyone who's still awake and ask them to read their favorite one-liner aloud. This book will turn anyone into a world-class wit.

There is a certain amount of wisdom and truth in these quips. Mark Twain, Bill Cosby, Dave Barry, Rita Rudner, Henny Youngman, Erma Bombeck, and Roseanne all would agree one thing: Laughing about getting older is a lot better than the alternative.

Bruce Lansky

**Life would be infinitely happier
if we could only be born at the age of eighty
and gradually approach eighteen.**
—Mark Twain

**Youth is a wonderful thing.
What a crime to waste it on children.**
—George Bernard Shaw

**Youth would be an ideal state
if it came a little later in life.**
—Lord Asquith

**When I was young,
the Dead Sea was still alive.**
—George Burns

I am not young enough to know everything.
—Oscar Wilde

**Youth is a disease
from which we all recover.**
—Dorothy Fuldheim

A man has reached middle age when he is
warned to slow down by his doctor
instead of the police.
—*Henny Youngman*

Middle age is having a choice of two
temptations and choosing the one that
will get you home earlier.
—*Dan Bennett*

Middle age is the time a guy
starts turning out lights for economic
rather than romantic reasons.
—*John Marino*

You know you're into middle age
when first you realize
that caution is the only thing
you care to exercise.
—*Charles Ghigna*

Middle age is when a narrow waist and a broad mind begin to change places.
—*Glenn Dorenbush*

Middle age is when your wife tells you to pull in your stomach, and you already have.
—*Jack Barry*

Middle age is when your age starts showing around your middle.
—*Bob Hope*

The really frightening thing about middle age
is the knowledge that you'll grow out of it.
—*Doris Day*

Middle age is when you realize
there's one more thing in the world
that's biodegradable—you.
—*Robert Orben*

Middle age is when anything new you feel
is most likely to be a symptom.
—*Laurence J. Peter*

"My mom and dad are still very sharp."

Middle age is when you know all the answers
and nobody asks you the questions.
—*Bob Phillips*

Middle age is when we can *do* just as much
as ever—but would rather not.
—*Anonymous*

Middle age is when the best exercise
is discretion.
—*Laurence J. Peter*

Middle age is when a man
is always thinking that in a week or two
he will feel as good as ever.
—*Don Marquis*

Middle age is when, no matter when you go
on holiday, you pack a sweater.
—*Denis Norden*

Middle age is when you still believe
you'll feel better in the morning.
—*Laurence J. Peter*

Senescence begins,
and middle age ends
the day your descendants
outnumber your friends.
—*Ogden Nash*

Middle age is when a woman's hair starts turning from gray to black.
—*Anonymous*

Years ago, we discovered the exact point, the dead center of middle age. It occurs when you are too young to take up golf and too old to rush up to the net.
—*Franklin P. Adams*

One of the chief pleasures of middle age is looking back at the people you didn't marry.
—*Anonymous*

*"There goes the picture tube.
Well, Mabel, how have you been the past few years?"*

The best thing that can happen to a couple
married for fifty years or more is that
they both grow nearsighted together.
—*Linda Fiterman*

I'm growing old by myself.
My wife hasn't had a birthday in years.
—*Milton Berle*

A diplomat is a man
who always remembers his wife's birthday
but never remembers her age.
—*Robert Frost*

To keep a happy marriage strong,
these thoughts you must engage;
remember your wife's birthday, but
forget to say her age.

—*Charles Ghigna*

I don't date women my age. There aren't any.
—*Milton Berle*

My grandmother's ninety. She's dating. He's ninety-three. It's going great. They never argue. They can't hear each other.
—*Cathy Ladman*

As an eighty-year-old woman, I only hear "woo, woo" when I'm riding in an ambulance.
—*Helen Ksypka*

At my age, when a girl flirts with me in the movies, she's after my popcorn.
—*Milton Berle*

I have my eighty-seventh birthday coming up and people ask me what I'd most appreciate getting. I'll tell you: a paternity suit.
—*George Burns*

At my age, "getting a little action" means I don't need to take a laxative.
—*Bruce Lansky*

"Your prescription has been taken care of by this gentleman."

It's hard for me to get used to these changing times. I can remember when the air was clean and sex was dirty.
—*George Burns*

I'm at the age where food has taken the place of sex in my life. In fact, I've just had a mirror put over my kitchen table.
—*Rodney Dangerfield*

Don't worry about avoiding temptation. As you grow older, it will avoid you.
—*Joey Adams*

As I grow older and older
and totter toward the tomb,
I find that I care less and less
who goes to bed with whom.
—Dorothy L. Sayers

Old age? That's the period of life when you buy a see-through nightgown and then remember you don't know anybody who can still see through one.
—*Bette Davis*

I'm getting old. When I squeeze into a tight parking space, I'm sexually satisfied for the day.
—*Rodney Dangerfield*

A man's sexuality goes through three stages: tri-weekly, try-weekly, and try-weakly.
—*Sydney Meltzer Klainhenz*

When we were young, you made me blush,
go hot and cold, and turn to mush.
I still feel all these things, it's true . . .
but is it menopause, or you?
—Susan D. Anderson

it's nice raising something that doesn't talk back to you...
Peas
ED FISCHER

Children are a great comfort in your old age,
and they help you reach it faster, too.
—*Lionel Kaufman*

We don't drink and drive.
Our kids always have the car.
—*Bumper sticker*

Be nice to your children,
for they will choose your rest home.
—*Phyllis Diller*

Our children inform us of wonderful things,
things that they feel we should know,
forgetting that those were the very same things
we taught them ourselves long ago.

—*Evelyn Amuedo Wade*

It's hard for the younger generation to understand Thoreau, who lived beside a pond but didn't own waterskis and a snorkel.
—*Bill Vaughan*

What's become of the younger generation? They've grown up and started worrying about the younger generation.
—*Roger Allen*

When I was young there was no respect for the young, and now that I am old there is no respect for the old. I missed out coming and going.
—*J. B. Priestly*

If I had known how wonderful it would be to have grandchildren, I'd have had them first.
—*Lois Wyse*

The good news is that grandchildren keep you young. The bad news is that after you spend time with them you feel your age.
—*Joan Holleman and Audrey Sherins*

The guy who wasn't smart enough to marry my daughter is the father of the smartest grandchild in the world.
—*Joey Adams*

Every time I try to take out a new lease on life, the landlord raises the rent.
—*Ashleigh Brilliant*

Today isn't the first day of the rest of your life. It's Tuesday.
—*Bruce Lansky and K. L. Jones*

Life's a tough proposition but the first hundred years are the hardest.
—*Wilson Mizner*

Life moves pretty fast; if you don't stop
and look around every once in a while,
you could miss it.
—*Matthew Broderick, Ferris Bueller's Day Off*

Life is what happens to you while you are
making other plans.
—*John Lennon*

Life is like a dog sled team. If you ain't the
lead dog, the scenery never changes.
—*Lewis Grizzard*

"On second thought, make that with onions."

Don't worry about tomorrow; who knows what will befall you today?
—*Yiddish folk saying*

The longer I live the less future there is to worry about.
—*Ashleigh Brilliant*

Life is ten percent what you make it and ninety percent how you take it.
—*Irving Berlin*

Life is far too important to ever talk
seriously about.
—*Oscar Wilde*

Life is like a grade-B movie.
You don't want to leave in the middle of it,
but you don't want to see it again.
—*Ted Turner*

Life is full of misery, loneliness, and
suffering—and it's all over much too soon.
—*Woody Allen*

Hope for the best.
Expect the worst.
Life is a play.
We're unrehearsed.
　　—Mel Brooks

Not only is life a bitch, it has puppies.
—*Adrienne E. Gusoff*

Life is just a bowl of pits.
—*Rodney Dangerfield*

Life is never fair, and perhaps it is a good thing for most of us that it is not.
—*Oscar Wilde*

**Don't take life so seriously . . .
it's not permanent.**
—*Kathy Holder*

**Why torture yourself
when life will do it for you?**
—*Laura Walker*

**Life is pleasant. Death is peaceful.
It's the transition that's troublesome.**
—*Isaac Asimov*

The only thing I regret about my life is the length of it. If I had to live my life again, I'd make all the same mistakes—only sooner.
—*Tallulah Bankhead*

My one regret in life is that I am not someone else.
—*Woody Allen*

Despite the cost of living, it's still quite popular.
—*Laurence J. Peter*

**Life can only be understood backwards,
but it must be lived forwards.**
—*Søren Kierkegaard*

The future isn't what it used to be.
—*Linda Moakes*

**Being a living legend is better
than being a dead legend.**
—*George Burns*

By the time a man is wise enough to watch his step, he's too old to go anywhere.
—*Joey Adams*

The trouble is, by the time you can read a girl like a book, your library card has expired.
—*Milton Berle*

By the time we've made it, we've had it.
—*Malcolm Forbes*

what's the matter – did I misplace the car keys again?
no – where's the car?

Experience is the name everyone gives
to their mistakes.
—*Oscar Wilde*

By the time you've figured out all the things
you shouldn't do, you've already done them.
—*Bruce Lansky*

Good judgment comes from experience,
and experience comes from bad judgment.
—*Barry LaPatner*

Experience teaches you to recognize
a mistake when you've made it again.
—*Anonymous*

If we could sell our experiences for what they
cost us, we'd be millionaires.
—*Abigail Van Buren*

If you don't learn from your mistakes,
someone else will.
—*Bruce Lansky and K. L. Jones*

Now that I can afford a big house, I don't
have the energy to clean it.
—*Denise Tiffany*

If you're old enough to know better,
you're too old to do it.
—*George Burns*

No one is ever old enough to know better.
—*Holbrook Jackson*

The old believe everything,
the middle-aged suspect everything,
the young know everything.
—*Oscar Wilde*

Middle age is when a woman on a train gets
up to offer her seat to you.
Old age is when the woman who gets up
to offer you her seat is pregnant.
—*Bruce Lansky*

Forty is the old age of youth;
fifty is the youth of old age.
—*French proverb*

"And how are your children doing at college?"

From birth to age eighteen, a girl needs good parents. From eighteen to thirty-five, she needs good looks. From thirty-five to fifty-five, she needs a good personality. From fifty-five on, she needs good cash.
—*Sophie Tucker*

You've heard of the three ages of man—youth, age, and "you're looking wonderful."
—*Francis Joseph, Cardinal Spellman*

The four stages of man are infancy, childhood, adolescence, and obsolescence.
—*Art Linkletter*

Remember, no matter how many candles you blow out this year, there's one gal who will always think of you as young, strong, and handsome—your mother.
—*Susan D. Anderson*

In the first twenty years of a man's life, his mother is always wondering where he's going. In the next twenty years, his wife wonders where he's been. Finally, when he dies, his friends wonder where he's at.
—*Lewis Grizzard*

It has begun to occur to me that life is a stage I'm going through.
—*Ellen Goodman*

Crossing the street in New York keeps old
people young—if they make it.
—*Andy Rooney*

You can't help getting older,
but you don't have to get old.
—*George Burns*

The secret to staying young is
to live honestly, eat slowly,
and lie about your age.
—*Lucille Ball*

I don't think I'll ever live to be a hundred.
I've been fifty for twenty years now.
—*Helen Ksypka*

I refuse to admit that I am more than
fifty-two, even if that does make
my sons illegitimate.
—*Nancy Astor*

Push-ups, sit-ups, run in place.
Each night I keep a grueling pace.
With bleak results, I must divulge—
I've lost the battle of the bulge.

—*Charles Ghigna*

After thirty, a body has a mind of its own.
—*Bette Midler*

The older you get, the harder it is to lose weight, because your body has made friends with your fat.
—*Lynn Alpern and Esther Blumenfeld*

As for me, except for an occasional heart attack, I feel as young as I ever did.
—*Robert Benchley*

It's not the fact that all my hair
is jumping ship in droves,
or that I hoard my medicines
like precious treasure troves.

It's not that once-true memory banks
will not cooperate,
or parts that once had muscle tone
now downward gravitate.

It's not the fact that I can't eat
the foods I used to love.
It's not a single one of these—
it's all of the above.

—Robert Scotellaro

You're aging when your actions
creak louder than your words.
—*Milton Berle*

Every year I get a little wi*d*ser.
—*Bruce Lansky*

I have long thought that the aging process
could be slowed down if it had to work its
way through Congress.
—*George Bush*

As we grow older, year by year,
my husband always mourns.
The less and less we feel our oats,
the more we feel our corns.
　　　　—*Evelyn Amuedo Wade*

Aging is a one-way street with no stop lights.
—*Babs Bell Hajdusiewicz*

Age is a question of mind over matter.
If you don't mind, it doesn't matter.
—*Satchel Paige*

Age is something that doesn't matter,
unless you are a cheese.
—*Billie Burke*

I have everything I had twenty years ago,
only it's all a little bit lower.
—*Gypsy Rose Lee*

I don't know how you feel about old age,
but in my case I didn't even see it coming.
It hit me from the rear.
—*Phyllis Diller*

The bad part is that you have to grow old
before somebody will tell you that you look
young for your age.
—*Milton Berle*

The face I see is furrowed now.
In fact, it's rather rutty.
Revlon and Clinique just won't do.
I need a can of putty.
　　　　—Jane Thomas Noland

"Quick! Your gut reaction."

The good thing about going to your
twenty-five-year high school reunion is that
you get to see all your old classmates.
The bad thing is that they get to see you.
　　　　—Anita Milner

If you look like your passport photo,
you're too ill to travel.
　　　　—Will Kommen

You're at that age when everything Mother Nature gave you, Father Time is taking away.
—*Milton Berle*

Time wounds all heels.
—*Jane Ace*

When you can finally afford the rings you want, you'd rather no one noticed your hands.
—*Lois Muehl*

I much prefer being over the hill
to being under it.
—*Bruce Lansky*

As long as you're over the hill,
you might as well enjoy the view.
—*Anonymous*

Just remember, once you're over the hill,
you begin to pick up speed.
—*Charles Schultz*

You know you're getting old when
getting lucky means you've found
your car in the parking lot.
—*Bruce Lansky*

You know you're getting old when
you're sitting in a rocker and
you can't get it started.
—*Milton Berle*

You know you're getting old when
"tying one on" means fastening your
MedicAlert bracelet.
—*Robert Scotellaro*

You know you're getting old when the best part of your day is over when your alarm clock goes off.
—*John Ross*

You know you're getting old when the candles cost more than the cake.
—*Bob Hope*

You know you're getting old when your toupee turns gray.
—*Milton Berle*

You know you're getting old when
your wife gives up sex for Lent, and you
don't realize it until the Fourth of July.
—*Milton Berle*

You're getting old when
you don't care where your wife goes,
just so you don't have to go along.
—*Henny Youngman*

You know you're getting old when the little
gray-haired lady you're helping across the
street is your wife.
—*John Ross*

You've reached old age when the gleam in your
eye is just the sun on your bifocals.
—*Henny Youngman*

I'll never make the mistake of being
seventy again.
—*Casey Stengel*

Anybody who says life begins at sixty must
have been asleep for the first fifty-nine years.
—*Lynne Alpern and Esther Blumenfeld*

Getting old has its advantages. I can no longer read the bathroom scale.
—*Brad Shreiber*

I used to dread getting older because I thought I would not be able to do all the things I wanted to do, but now that I am older I find that I don't want to do them.
—*Nancy Astor*

Old age isn't so bad when you consider the alternatives.
—*Maurice Chevalier*

*Old age is when you really don't care
what the neighbors think.*

Old age is when you need a nap
after dialing a long-distance call.
—*Bruce Lansky*

Old age is when you know all the answers but
nobody asks you the questions.
—*Anonymous*

You know you're getting old when all
the names in your black book
have an M.D. after them.
—*Arnold Palmer*

71

I don't feel eighty. In fact, I don't feel
anything till noon. Then it's time for my nap.
—*Bob Hope*

I'm at the age now where just putting
my cigar in its holder is a thrill.
—*George Burns*

I smoke cigars because at my age
if I don't have something to hang on to,
I might fall down.
—*George Burns*

They bit and chewed and served me well
as through the years we ventured.
We had a falling out, and now
my new teeth are indentured.
   —Sydnie Meltzer Kleinhenz

The only way to keep your health is to eat what you don't want, drink what you don't like, and do what you'd rather not.
—*Mark Twain*

The cardiologist's diet:
if it tastes good, spit it out.
—*Paulina Borsook*

Doctors are men who prescribe medicines of which they know little, to cure diseases of which they know less, in human beings of whom they know nothing.
—*Voltaire*

I'm scared of dentists' needles,
I'm scared of dentists' drills,
but even more than fear of pain,
I'm scared of dentists' bills.
—*Bruce Lansky*

"Frankly, Robert, I find it hard to put complete confidence in someone I once had to flunk out of ninth-grade math."

Old people shouldn't eat health foods.
They need all the preservatives they can get.
—*Robert Orben*

When I was forty, my doctor advised me that
a man in his forties shouldn't play tennis.
I heeded his advice carefully and could hardly
wait until I reached fifty to start again.
—*Hugo Black*

My doctor gave me two weeks to live.
I hope they're in August.
—*Ronnie Shakes*

My uncle Max went to see his doctor.
The doctor gave him six months to live.
But my uncle couldn't pay his bill,
so the doctor gave him six more months.
—*Anonymous*

A doctor said to a little old man,
"You're going to live until you're sixty."
He said, "I am sixty."
The doctor said, "What did I tell you?"
—*Henny Youngman*

My doctor's very economical. If you can't
afford an operation, he'll touch up the x-rays.
—*Anonymous*

I feel so bad for Uncle Ted.
There's not much hair upon his head.
And, what is worse, he barely hears.
There's too much hair inside his ears.

—*Bruce Lansky*

After a certain age, if you don't wake up
aching in every joint, you are probably dead.
—*Tommy Mein*

My health is good; it's my age that's bad.
—*Roy Acuff*

I'm at an age where my back
goes out more than I do.
—*Phyllis Diller*

DAVE CARPENTER...

"I have good news and bad news.
The good news, you're not a hypochondriac . . . ."

The secret of longevity is to keep breathing.
—*Bruce Lansky*

First thing I do when I wake up in the morning is breathe on a mirror and hope it fogs.
—*Earl Wynn*

It is better to wear out than to rust out.
—*Richard Cumberland*

Another candle on your cake?
Well, that's no cause to pout.
Be glad that you have strength enough
to blow the damn thing out.
—*William R. Evans III & Andrew Frothingham*

My grandmother is
over eighty and still doesn't need glasses.
Drinks right out of the bottle.
—*Henny Youngman*

Quit worrying about your health. It'll go away.
—*Robert Orben*

I believe every human has a finite number of
heartbeats. I don't intend to waste any of
mine running around doing exercises.
—*Neil Armstrong*

*"Can't quite make it out, Mrs. Gurnbach?
And we drove here all by ourselves, did we?*

I adore my bifocals,
my false teeth fit fine,
my hairpiece looks good,
but I sure miss my mind.

—*Anonymous*

"Don't worry about senility,"
my grandfather used to say.
"When it hits you, you won't know it."
—*Bill Cosby*

There are three signs of old age:
loss of memory . . . I forget the other two.
—*Red Skelton*

It's hard to be nostalgic when you can't
remember anything.
—*Anonymous*

*"Could we please get through one dinner party
without the jokes about my memory?"*

First you forget names, then you forget faces, then you forget to pull your zipper up, then you forget to pull your zipper down.
—*Leo Rosenberg*

At my age I don't care if my mind starts to wander—just as long as it comes back again.
—*Mike Knowles*

The older I grow the more I distrust the familiar doctrine that age brings wisdom.
—*H.L. Mencken*

My grandmother started walking five miles a day when she was sixty. She's ninety-seven now, and we don't know where the hell she is.

—*Ellen DeGeneris*

My grandfather's a little forgetful, but he likes to give me advice. One day he took me aside and left me there.

—*Ron Richards*

Nostalgia isn't what it used to be.
—*Simone Signoret*

An old-timer is one who can remember when a juvenile delinquent was a kid who owed eight cents on an overdue library book.
—*Leonard Louis Levinson*

The older a man gets, the farther he had to walk to school as a boy.
—*Anonymous*

I'm so old that bartenders check my pulse instead of my ID.

—*Louise Bowie*

He's so old that when he orders a three-minute egg, they ask for the money up front.

—*Milton Berle*

You know you're getting old when you stop buying green bananas.

—*Lewis Grizzard*

Very, very, very few
people die at ninety-two.
I suppose that I shall be
safer still at ninety-three.

—*Willard R. Espy*

Anyone can get old.
All you have to do is live long enough.
—*Groucho Marx*

There's one advantage to being 102—
no peer pressure.
—*Dennis Wolfberg*

If you survive long enough, you're revered—
rather like an old building.
—*Katherine Hepburn*

*"Then it's moved and seconded that the compulsory
retirement age be advanced to ninety-five."*

I'm not afraid to die. I just don't want to be
there when it happens.
—*Woody Allen*

Death is not the end. There remains the
litigation over the estate.
—*Ambrose Bierce*

Death is nature's way of telling you
to slow down.
—*Graffiti*

I am ready to meet my maker. Whether my maker is prepared for the ordeal of meeting me is another matter.
—*Winston Churchill*

What! You've been keeping records on me? I wasn't so bad! How many times did I take the Lord's name in vain? A million and six? Jesus Ch—!
—*Steve Martin*

I don't believe in an afterlife, although I am bringing a change of underwear.
—*Woody Allen*

It costs me never a stab or squirm
to tread by chance upon a worm.
"Aha, my little dear," I say,
"Your clan will pay me back one day."
—Dorothy Parker

They say such nice things about people
at their funerals that it makes
me sad to realize that I'm going
to miss mine by just a few days.
—*Garrison Keillor*

The best way to get praise is to die.
—*Italian proverb*

I don't want to achieve immortality by being
inducted into baseball's hall of fame.
I want to achieve immortality by not dying.
—*Leo Durocher*

do you take this woman til death do you part?
no problem
ED FISCHER

The reports of my death
are greatly exaggerated.
—*Mark Twain*

Two elders meet on a street corner
downtown. One says to the other,
"Gosh, I haven't seen you in years.
I can't seem to remember—
was it you or your brother who died?"
—*Jane Thomas Noland*

Early to rise and early to bed makes
a male healthy and wealthy and dead.
—*James Thurber*

I get up each morning and dust off my wits,
then pick up the paper and read the "o-bits."
If my name isn't there, then I know I'm not dead.
I eat a good breakfast and go back to bed.

—*Anonymous*

My uncle Pat, he read the death column every morning in the paper. And he can't understand how people always die in alphabetical order.
—*Hal Roach*

Last Will and Testament: Being of sound mind, I spent all my money.
—*Anonymous*

Big deal! I'm used to dust.
—*Erma Bombeck's requested gravestone epitaph*

INDEX

Also from Meadowbrook Press

✦ ***Golf's Funniest Anecdotes***
This collection of 185 true and funny anecdotes about famous golfers, including Chi Chi Rodriguez, Lee Travino, Tiger Woods, Arnold Palmer, and Jack Nicklaus, is sure to get any golfer chuckling.

✦ ***The Joy of...Series***
Six treasuries of wise and warm advice for that special parent, grandparent, spouse, sister, or friend in your life. These collections reflect the wittiest and wisest (and sometimes most amusing) sentiments ever written about those whom we hold most dear. Each book is illustrated with black-and-white photographs that poignantly depict the unique relationships between family and friends. These books are the perfect gift to show a loved one how much you care. *The Joy of Cats, Joy of Friendship, Joy of Grandparenting, Joy of Marriage, Joy of Parenthood*, and *Joy of Sisters*.

✦ ***What You Don't Know About Retirement***
"**Q**: How can I make sure my friends and family stay in touch? **A**: Move to a vacation spot and live in a place with a pool. **Q**: Why is it dangerous for a retiree to miss the condo-owners association meeting? **A**: They might be elected president." Makes a great gift and provides a funny quiz to make any retirement party more fun.

We offer many more titles written to delight, inform, and entertain.
To order books with a credit card or browse our full
selection of titles, visit our web site at:

www.meadowbrookpress.com

or call toll-free to place an order, request a free catalog, or ask a question:

1-800-338-2232

Meadowbrook Press • 5451 Smetana Drive • Minnetonka, MN • 55343